Revolution

A Creative Writing Project based on the Revolutionary War

By Susan Kemmerer

Schoolhouse Publishing
659 Schoolhouse Road
Telford, PA 18969
www.shpublishing.com

Published by
Schoolhouse Publishing
659 Schoolhouse Road
Telford, PA 18969
www.shpublishing.com

Waiver of Responsibility

It is important to use **Revolution** in conjunction with individual course work. Because the results of using this guide will differ from student to student, the author may not be held responsible for the educational outcome.

© 2002 by Susan KemmererAll rights reserved. No part of this publication may be reproduced, stored in a retrieval system, or transmitted in any form or by any means without prior permission of Schoolhouse Publishing, except for individual copies for use within a family by immediate family members.

Dedication

To my fourth son, Joshua. Thank you for so gamely trying my new book ("Oh, no! Mom's having another one of her brainstorms!") You are such an encouragement to me – and such a wonderful helper. Thank you! We named you after the Joshua of the Bible – and you are learning, in the Lord, to be strong and courageous – just like your biblical namesake. I love you.

Also to Dwayne and Chris, who were among my original guinea pigs. But I won't say any more, because I already dedicated books to you. I love you.

And to my husband, Dale, who is always so supportive of me and my brainstorms. I love you.

And to Jesus Christ, my Lord and Savior, who always enables me to apply creativity (even when I felt I had no creativity left) to our homeschool in each situation uniquely for each precious child He has entrusted to me. I love you.

To The Teacher

    Have you ever tried to teach on a subject so vast, so grand, that you found yourself unable to impart your excitement and inspiration to your students? It's so frustrating! That's how I felt as we were studying the period of American history covering the Revolutionary War. What I found to be awe-inspiring, my students found to be boring! Where I saw God's mighty hand at work doing mighty things, my students were glazing over! In my frustration I prayed that God would help me to reveal to my students His awesome acts as we studied. This book is the result.
    My objective was for my students to try to re-enact those days in the guise of a creative writing project. The subject: Create your own country. I wanted them to *think* the thoughts the Founding Fathers thought. In the process, my students would hopefully be awed and overwhelmed with gratefulness to God for their heritage.
    As you work through the pages of this book, keep in mind that in reality we should never experience another Revolution. The Civil War settled, once and for all, the question of whether or not a state could secede from the Union.

    Please Note: Since you *don't* want to stir up discontent or anti-national sentiment in your students, *please* remind them that this is a *historic* exercise with current-day flavor so that our students can relate more readily. To further cement this differentiation in the minds of your students, you may want to insist that they use an imaginary country as the "mother country." My prayer is that your students will be moved to worship God as they seek to recreate the events of the American Revolution in their own time reference and in their own words.

                                    -Susan Kemmerer
                                    Author

How To Use This Guide

This guide is very, very easy to use. You will accomplish an amazing feat through the pages of this guide! You will create an entire country, step-by-step, while following the example of our Founding Fathers.

Start with Lesson 1. Follow the instructions. Some of the lessons need to be evaluated by your teacher when you are through. Your teacher will decide whether you achieved your objective or not, and will tell you where to go from there. For example, if you win the court case in Lesson 4, you will proceed to Lesson 5. If you lose your court case, you will proceed to Lesson 6. Don't worry. Everything is carefully explained.

Please Note: Many of the lessons have notes to help make the project easier to understand. If you are directed to check the notes in the appendix, make sure that you do so.

My prayer is that you will gain a better understanding of and appreciation for your heritage. Don't forget to spend time in prayer thanking God for the blessing He has given you as a citizen of this great country!

Lesson 1

Something is stirring in your spirit. You love your country, but you are frustrated by all that you see around you. You feel as if there is a decline morally, politically, socially, and economically. Now it is falling upon your shoulders to stop the decline. You must make a difference.

Assignment

You will need to assess the current condition of your country. In particular, describe the things you see that are wrong with it. You will want to include an analysis on religious, economic, educational, political, and social conditions. Thoughtfully fill out the assessment sheet on the following page.

And You Think You Have It Bad...

Britain had just been in a costly war against France. Part of this war was fought in the colonies and was known as the French and Indian Wars. Consequently, the British felt that the colonists should foot the bill for part of the war.

King George believed that the colonists needed to understand who was ruling whom – they needed to be taught a lesson.

For these reasons:
- Taxes were levied against many everyday items such as paper, paint, and tea.
- Colonists had to allow British soldiers to live in their homes.
- Colonists had to feed British soldiers.
- Colonists weren't allowed to print anything expressing their negative opinions about British policy or the King.
- Colonists weren't allowed to hold any meetings that were for the purpose of achieving justice for the situation.
- Public grounds were used by the British for training and drilling their soldiers.

Assessment

1. In what ways have freedoms been eroded in your country in the following areas. Be specific.
    - Religion: _____

    - Education: _____

    - Politics: _____

    - Economics: _____

    - Social/Family: _____

2. In what ways are our taxes being used to foster these problems? _____

3. In what ways are the people being "brainwashed" to accept these conditions: _____

4. Which of the problems described above do you see as the most significant and why: _____

Lesson 2

As you have demonstrated, the conditions in this country have deteriorated. It is the unfortunate condition of sinful man. But, you are being stirred up. Isn't it possible that something can be done to arrest the decline? If you can rally enough like-minded people, perhaps something can be done!

Assignment

Based on the information you wrote in your country analysis, you will create a campaign to educate the people of your country about the problems you have seen. You will be setting up an organization for the purpose of changing the problems.

- **Day 1** – Do the assignments on page 4.
- **Day 2** – Do the assignment on page 5.
- **Day 3** – Do the assignment on page 6.
- **Day 4** – Do the assignment on page 7.

The Liberty Tree

The Liberty Tree became a symbol throughout the colonies of freedom. Organized groups met under these large trees to pass on information and to plan their agendas. The Liberty Tree has been memorialized on Connecticut's state quarter.

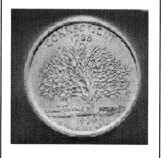

Get Organized

In order to change the problems in your country, you must connect all the like-minded people, educate the population, and work toward change. To accomplish this, you will need to create an organization. **(See note, page 54.)**

The name of your organization: _____

Your organization's slogan: _____
_____
_____

In the space below, create a button and a bumper sticker to promote your cause:

Sons of Liberty

The cause of freedom was at stake just before the Revolutionary War. In an effort to organize, Samuel Adams started several organizations, the most famous being the *Sons of Liberty*.

The Sons of Liberty sometimes acted legally, fighting in courts and through newspapers to promote liberty. Sometimes the Sons of Liberty acted illegally, using vandalism, harassment, and threats to further their cause.

Extra, Extra, Read All About It!

Write a letter to the editor of an imaginary newspaper. In your letter explain you position on various issues. Tell about your organization. Give details of how interested readers can contact you. Don't forget to explain what your organization believes in!

Committees of Correspondence

Before the Revolution, prominent men in each of the colonies realized the need to correspond with other colonial leaders. They needed advice from each other on how to wisely govern and how to deal with British excesses. They needed to unite.

Samuel Adams organized Committees of Correspondence to meet this need. Without an effective postal system, telephone, or other modern methods of communication, the Committees helped to "get the word out."

The leaders who formed the Committees later became the first Continental Congress – and also were leaders in the Revolution. They included men like Samuel Adams, Patrick Henry, and Thomas Jefferson.

Uncle Sam Wants YOU

The success of any organization is dependent on its *human resources*. Without good people you aren't going to get anywhere. Although it is important to attract lots of people, you also need people who are dedicated, intelligent, hardworking, and courageous. It is your job to sort through the many applications you have received and to pick two people to lead your organization. What makes these two people *ideal* ? You may describe imaginary people or describe two people you actually know that you believe would benefit your organization. **(See note, page 54.)**

Thomas Jefferson

You couldn't find a more brilliant, hardworking man than Tom Jefferson. Besides being a leader in the Revolution, during his lifetime he was a farmer, a lawyer, a burgess, an ambassador, secretary of state, inventor, writer (he wrote the Declaration of Independence), creator of the dollar, president of the United States, and he doubled the size of the United States during his presidency.

Tom was definitely someone to have on your side!

Committee Chairman

_____
_____
_____
_____
_____
_____
_____
_____
_____
_____
_____
_____

Committee Vice Chairman

_____
_____
_____
_____
_____
_____
_____
_____
_____
_____
_____
_____

John Hancock

If you wanted to get things done, you could certainly count on John Hancock. He was a real "people person." He was the second richest man in America. During his lifetime he served as selectman, a Massachusetts delegate, president of the Continental Congress, a major in the Massachusetts militia, and Governor of Massachusetts. He also ran an extensive shipping business. King George III placed John Hancock at the top of his "List of the Most Dangerous Americans" and put a price on John's head. But this didn't stop John Hancock!

John would be an asset to any organization!

Gettin' The Job Done

As an organization, you have a lot to accomplish. You need to educate the public. You have to work to change things. You have to stop your opponents. Below, describe some of the methods you employ to get the job done. You may be factual or write it in story form.

To Obey... Or Not To Obey- That is the Question!

During the period of time just before the Revolution, the colonists employed many methods to get the job done. Many of their methods were legal, but many were illegal.

Many of the leaders of the Revolution were Christians. Choosing to use illegal methods to further their cause must have been a difficult decision to make. Of course, some of their legal activities changed to illegal activities as the King grew angrier.

What were some of their methods? Here are a few of their ideas: newspaper articles, demonstrations, church sermons, court appeals, tar and feathering, smuggling, creating and arming a militia, vandalism, and parades.

Tea, Anyone?

The Boston Tea Party was a mass demonstration created by Boston's Revolution leaders. When King George insisted the tea on the ships had to be unloaded and the tax paid, Boston officials refused. For 20 days Boston's leaders used legal methods (like appeals to the Governor) to turn the ships back. Nothing worked.

On December 16, 1773, some 50 men dressed as Indians boarded three ships and threw the taxed tea into the harbor.

Teacher's note: Please read through the assignment on this page. If your student chose legal methods for his organization, proceed to lesson 3 on page 8. If your student chose illegal methods, proceed to lesson 4 on page 11.

Lesson 3

Boston Massacre?

In March of 1770 a British sentry became the target of some colonial troublemakers. They pushed and shoved the guard and threw rocks and iced snowballs at him. The guard yelled for help, and nine more British soldiers came to his rescue.

The mob grew larger and more violent, hitting the soldiers with sticks and taunting them, "We dare you to fire!"

One soldier thought the words were an order from his commander and he opened fire on the "unarmed" crowd. This really angered the mob, and they pressed threateningly forward.

The panicked soldiers fired repeatedly into the angry mob, killing 5 Americans and wounding others.

Question: So, who was at fault? Who was guilty of what?

> "The one who states his case first seems right, until the other comes and examines him."
> Proverbs 18: 17

Your wise handling of your organization has generated great interest. People are noticing – and signing up in huge numbers! The organized groups that are opposed to your ideals are also noticing – and have decided to take you to court to stop you. After all, the law *is* on their side.

There is no reason to fear. This just gives you an opportunity to set legal precedent and possibly change the laws in your state. After all, the people *are* on your side.

Assignment

Create the case. You must intelligently present *both sides* of the court case – theirs as well as yours. Remember, there are always two sides to a case.

Answer

One of the most learned men in the colonies was a godly man, a lawyer, named John Adams. He believed that it was vastly important for the colonies to *prove* they could justly and fairly govern themselves. He insisted on a fair trial for the soldiers of the Boston Massacre.

Adams volunteered to defend the soldiers (even though he, himself, was a patriot). He argued that the soldiers had acted in self-defense.

Thanks to his efforts, six of the soldiers were found "not guilty," and two were found guilty of a lesser charge, manslaughter. Their punishment? Branding.

John Adams later became our country's third president.

Hear Ye! Hear Ye!

Famous Supreme Court cases such as Roe vs. Wade have changed the course of history. In a court case, generally one side has a biblical foundation and the other side has a "selfish" foundation. As our country moves away from its Christian roots, more and more cases are won by those who are selfishly founded rather than biblically founded.

On this sheet you will present *their* side of the case *against* your organization and its methods. (**See note on page 54.**)

This is the case of _____ **vs.** _____.
(their organization)   (your organization)

State *their* interpretation of the law (use your "Assessment" sheet from lesson 1, page 2, to help you). _____

State the "freedoms" they want to keep "intact." _____

State the "evidence" they have against you: _____

State any new "freedoms" they want to legalize through this case, and explain these freedoms from *their* point of view: _____

State any "restrictions" they want to impose on your organization through this case: _____

Go on to the next page...

Hear Ye! Hear Ye!

This is a classic battle that has continued throughout history: two sides both wanting more freedom. But, freedom granted to one side is often freedom denied the other (sometimes rightly). By granting women the freedom to choose abortion, our country has denied the unborn the freedom to live. By granting freedom to slaves, slaveowners were denied freedom to own "property" and to run their businesses without government intervention.

On this sheet you will present *your* side of the case. (**See note on page 54.**)

State your interpretation of the law (use your "Assessment" sheet from lesson 1, page 2, to help you). _____
_____
_____
_____

State the "freedoms" you want to keep "intact." _____
_____
_____

Explain the "evidence" they have against you: _____
_____
_____
_____
_____

State any new "freedoms" you want to legalize through this case, and explain these freedoms from *your* point of view: _____
_____
_____
_____

State any "restrictions" you want to impose on their organization through this case: _____
_____
_____
_____

Teacher's note: Please read through the assignment on these two pages (9-10). If your student won his court case in your opinion, proceed to lesson 5, page 14. If your student lost his court case, proceed to lesson 6, page 16.

Lesson 4

> "The one who states his case first seems right, until the other comes and examines him."
> Proverbs 18: 17

The Case of the Spy

Nathan Hale was a well-educated man. He was a soldier – a lieutenant – in the army of Connecticut under General George Washington. Most importantly, he was a very brave man.

General Washington could not win the war unless he could find what the British were up to. He needed spies…and Nathan bravely volunteered.

Before long, Nathan was caught by the British and arrested for his illegal activities.

Question: So what do you do with a spy? What would *you* do if you caught a spy in your organization?

Your organization has chosen illegal methods to further your agenda. Accordingly, you have been arrested. You have lost your case in the lower courts and have successfully appealed to a higher court. This gives you an opportunity to set legal precedent and possibly to change the laws in your state.

Assignment

You must defend yourself in court. If you lose, your organization could be shut down. You must intelligently argue *both* sides of the case.

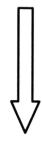

The conclusion...

British military law required spies to be immediately executed – without a trial. Thus, Nathan Hale was hung as a spy and died for his country.

What were his final words? "My only regret is that I have only one life to give for my country."

Hear Ye! Hear Ye!

Famous Supreme Court cases such as Roe vs. Wade have changed the course of history. In a court case, generally one side has a biblical foundation and the other side has a "selfish" foundation. As our country moves away from its Christian roots, more and more cases are won by those who are selfishly founded rather than biblically founded.

On this sheet you will present *their* side of the case against your organization and its methods. (**See note on page 54.**)

This is the case of _____ vs. _____.
　　　　　　　　　　　　(their organization)　　(your organization)

State *their* interpretation of the law (use your "Assessment" sheet from lesson 1, page 2, to help you). _____

State the "freedoms" they want to keep "intact." _____

State the "evidence" they have against you: _____

State any new "freedoms" they want to legalize through this case, and explain these freedoms from *their* point of view: _____

State any "restrictions" they want to impose on your organization through this case: _____

Go on to the next page... ⟶

Hear Ye! Hear Ye!

This is a classic battle that has continued throughout history: two sides both wanting more freedom. But, freedom granted to one side is often freedom denied the other (sometimes rightly). By granting women the freedom to chose abortion, our country has denied the unborn the freedom to live. By granting freedom to slaves, slaveowners were denied freedom to own "property" and to run their businesses without government intervention.

On this sheet you will present *your* side of the case. (**See note on page 54.**)

State your interpretation of the law (use your "Assessment" sheet from lesson 1, page 2, to help you). _____
_____
_____
_____

State the "freedoms" you want to keep "intact." _____
_____
_____

Explain the "evidence" they have against you: _____
_____
_____
_____
_____

State any new "freedoms" you want to legalize through this case, and explain these freedoms from *your* point of view: _____
_____
_____
_____

State any "restrictions" you want to impose on their organization through this case: _____
_____
_____
_____

Teacher's note: Please read through the assignment on these two pages (12,13). If your student won his court case in your opinion, proceed to lesson 5, page 14. If your student lost his court case, proceed to lesson 6, page 16.

Lesson 5

> **From God??**
>
> "Let every soul be subject to the governing authorities. For there is no authority except from God, and the authorities that exist are appointed by God."
>
> Romans 13:1

Congratulations! You won your case! Although this is great news for your side, the opposition is really up in arms about your victory. They have begun to harass you in many stealthy ways – and no one seems to be able to catch them!

Thankfully, it will soon be election time. Your organization is grooming a candidate to run for Governor in the upcoming election. You are hoping he'll be strong enough to further your agenda *and* stop the opposition once and for all.

> **You want me to do what???**
>
> "Therefore I exhort first of all that supplications, prayers, intercessions, and giving of thanks be made for all men, for kings and all who are in authority, that we may lead a quiet and peaceable life in all godliness and reverence."
>
> 1 Timothy 2:1.2

Assignment

In the next assignment you will announce your candidate to the public.

Vote Smart!

This assignment will help you to create your candidate for governor. (**See note on page 55**.)

Your candidate's name:
_____

Age: _____

Describe your candidate's family (Is he/she married with children?):
_____
_____
_____
_____

In this box you will paste a picture of your candidate. Look through magazines to find a picture that represents the way your candidate looks. Keep in mind that appearance is, unfortunately, important to many people. A candidate that appears slovenly, play-boyish, or ignorant, even if he is very organized, capable, and intelligent, will have a hard time overcoming his outward appearance in the eyes of an appearance-worshipping society. Choose the appearance of your candidate carefully.

"For the LORD sees not as man sees: man looks on the outward appearance, but the LORD looks on the heart."
1 Samuel 16:7B ESV

Describe your candidate's education and job experience that qualify him for the job:
_____
_____
_____
_____
_____

How will your candidate change things in your state if he wins the election? What is his philosophy?
_____
_____
_____
_____
_____
_____
_____
_____

Create a campaign button in the circle above.

Teacher's note: Please read through the assignment on this page. If, in your opinion, your student's candidate won the election, proceed to lesson 7 on page 18. If your student's candidate lost, proceed to lesson 8 on page 23.

Lesson 6

From God??

"Let every soul be subject to the governing authorities. For there is no authority except from God, and the authorities that exist are appointed by God."
Romans 13:1

Our Condolences. You lost your case. Although this is great news for your opposition, you are really up in arms about their victory. You must make a last-ditch effort to win. You have decided to harass them in many stealthy ways – and no one seems to be able to catch you – in order to gain more sympathy and visibility.

Thankfully, it will soon be election time. Your organization is grooming a candidate to run for Governor in the upcoming election. You are hoping he'll be strong enough to further your agenda *and* stop the opposition. This election is your final opportunity.

You want me to do what???

"Therefore I exhort first of all that supplications, prayers, intercessions, and giving of thanks be made for all men, for kings and all who are in authority, that we may lead a quiet and peaceable life in all godliness and reverence."
1 Timothy 2:1,2

Assignment

In the next assignment you will announce your candidate to the public.

Vote Smart!

This assignment will help you to create your candidate for governor. (**See note on page 55**.)

Your candidate's name:

_____

Age: _____

Describe your candidate's family (Is he/she married with children?):

_____
_____
_____

Describe your candidate's education and job experience that qualify him for the job:

_____
_____
_____
_____

> In this box you will paste a picture of your candidate. Look through magazines to find a picture that represents the way your candidate looks. Keep in mind that appearance is, unfortunately, important to many people. A candidate that appears slovenly, play-boyish, or ignorant, even if he is very organized, capable, and intelligent, will have a hard time overcoming his outward appearance in the eyes of an appearance-worshipping society. Choose the appearance of your candidate carefully.
>
> "For the LORD sees not as man sees: man looks on the outward appearance, but the LORD looks on the heart."
> 1 Samuel 16:7B ESV

How will your candidate change things in your state if he wins the election? What is his philosophy?

_____
_____
_____
_____
_____
_____
_____
_____

Create a campaign button in the circle above.

Teacher's note: Please read through the assignment on this page. If, in your opinion, your student's candidate won the election, proceed to lesson 7 on page 18. If your student's candidate lost, proceed to lesson 8 on page 23.

Lesson 7

Could This Happen Now?

No! The Civil War settled the question once and for all. States cannot break away to form their own country. Read Article 1, Section 8, of the Constitution on page 32.

How Did It All Begin?

As tension mounted between the British and the colonials, it became more apparent that war was imminent. The colonials began to stockpile weapons and ammunition. They hid these stockpiles in the town of Concord.

When the British discovered the stockpile, they decided to march into Concord and seize it. The colonial minutemen tried to stop the British in the neighboring town of Lexington, but the British soldiers opened fire, killing several Americans. The date was April 19, 1775. That fateful event was known as "the shot heard around the world."

Frightening Reality

"I could get arrested for this!" –
   The sober words of one student after completing the assignment on Day 1.

* * *I * * * * *

And **THAT** is exactly what our Founding Fathers faced!

Congratulations! Your candidate won the election! Unfortunately the opposition is furious. They demand a recount. They stage a massive demonstration. Some of their people get out of hand and begin shooting paintballs at your defeated leadership team.

Believing themselves to be under attack, and not realizing that their "weapons" were essentially harmless, some of your soldiers open fire on the angry mob, killing and wounding a number of them. Retaliatory acts of violence are occurring more frequently. You are now so busy dealing with the violence, your new government has little time left over to push forward your agenda.

Your leadership team comes to the sobering conclusion that the only solution is to break away and start over – a whole new country. Let the opposition have the old one.

Assignment

Declare independence from the mother country and begin the process of creating a new country. **(Please see note on page 55.)**

- ❑ **Day 1** – Draft your Declaration of Independence on page 20, and write your final copy on page 21.
- ❑ **Day 2** – Make a map of your new country.

The Declaration of Independence – Paraphrased

When, in the course of human events, it becomes necessary for one government to dissolve old political ties for the purpose of becoming a separate and equal nation as entitled by God, then decency requires them to declare the reason for the separation.

We hold these truths to be self-evident: that all men are created equal; that they are endowed by their Creator with certain unalienable rights; that among these are life, liberty, and the pursuit of happiness. Governments are instituted among men to secure these rights. Governments receive their power from the consent of the people they govern. When any government becomes destructive of these ends, it is the right of the people to change or abolish it, and to institute a new government in the manner most likely to secure their safety and happiness.

The history of the present King of Great Britain is a history of repeated injuries and usurping of power. His agenda is to establish an absolute tyranny over these states. To prove this, we submit the following:

- He refuses to approve our good and necessary laws.
- He refuses to allow his governors to pass laws unless they get his permission – yet he constantly ignores them so they can't get the permission required.
- He refuses us representation in his government.
- He calls government meetings at inconvenient, distant places, making it impossible for us to attend.
- He dissolves our governments.
- He won't allow new governments to be voted in, leaving us ungoverned.
- He is preventing further immigration to the colonies.
- He won't set up a justice system.
- He keeps judges in his power by controlling their jobs and salaries.
- He creates multitudes of unnecessary jobs for his people, then forces us to support them.
- He keeps troops here in times of peace, without our consent.
- He established martial law.
- He established his own laws contrary to our laws.
- He forced us to quarter large numbers of his troops.
- He protected his troops from penalty of our law.
- He cut off our world trade.
- He taxed us without our consent.
- He refuses us trial by jury.
- He forces us to go to England for trials.
- He enlarged Canada's borders to force his will on us.
- He took away our state charters.
- He stopped our legislatures.
- He declared war against us.
- He plundered our seas and coastlines, burned our towns, and destroyed our people.
- He sent large armies and allied with other countries and peoples to destroy us.
- He has pirated our ships, forcing them to fight against us.
- He has stirred up the Indians against us.
- We have throughout all this appealed humbly to him, and he has ignored us.

We, therefore, appealing to God – the Supreme Judge of the world – do, in the name of the people, declare: these united colonies are free and independent states. We are absolved from all allegiance to the British crown. All political connections between us are totally dissolved. As free and independent states, we have full power to make war, peace, and alliances. We can establish trade. We may do all other activities that free independent states may do. To support this declaration we pledge our lives, our fortunes, and our sacred honor, as we rely on God for protection.

Your Declaration of Independence

Your declaration of independence is a legal document, drafted by your leadership team, in which you declare your independence from the mother country. After reading the paraphrase of the American Declaration of Independence on page 19, draft your own Declaration of Independence using the outline below (this will be your rough draft) Feel free to use some of the ideas of our Founding Fathers:

Look at the first two paragraphs of the Declaration on page 19. What do *you* believe are your *most basic* human rights? List them here: _____
_____

What do *you* believe are the *most basic* duties of government? Use the first two paragraphs, again, from page 19 for ideas. List your ideas here: _____
_____

Using your most eloquent language, write a paragraph stating your basic human rights and the duties of government (use the two lists you just composed above to help formulate your paragraph): _____
_____
_____
_____

Write a *sentence* stating that the rights and duties spoken of above have been violated (see the 3rd paragraph of the Declaration on page 19 as an example): _____
_____

Make a list demonstrating how the rights and duties listed in paragraph one of *your* declaration have been violated (see list on page 19 as an example):
- _____
- _____
- _____
- _____
- _____
- _____
- _____

In your most eloquent language, declare your independence from the mother country (use the final paragraph of the Declaration on page 19 as a model if you need help): _____
_____
_____
_____
_____
_____

On the next page, you will recopy your rough draft to create your final draft of your declaration of independence.

Declaration of Independence

Signed

Map It

22

Create your new country. Below you will need to indicate which portion of your state or which state(s) have broken away to form a new nation. Sketch in the boundaries of your new nation on the map below. Be strategic! Keep in mind such things as industrial centers, agricultural areas, major population centers, waterways, natural geographic protection (such as mountains), and borders of neighboring countries. **(Please see note on page 55.)**

Your new country's name: _____

Your new capital: _____ (indicate where it is located on your map by marking your new capital with a star)

Strategically explain your choice of boundaries for your new country: _____
_____

Create a Key for your Country
(Some of the areas that you shade on the map above will overlap one another.)

- On the map, major industrial centers are shaded like this: [ ]

- Major agricultural areas are shaded like this: [ ]

- Major population centers are shaded like this: [ ]

- Major waterways are indicated like this: [ ]

- Natural geographic protection is afforded by mountains: [ ] deserts: [ ]

Teacher's note: Please read through the assignment on this page. Did your student choose his country strategically? Discuss your opinion with your student, then proceed to lesson 9, page 24.

Lesson 8

Unfortunately, you were unable to gain the support of the majority, and your candidate lost the election. In response, your organization demands a recount. You stage a massive demonstration.

Some of your supporters get out of hand and shoot paintballs at the soldiers and police. Believing themselves to be under attack, they shoot into the crowd. Some are killed and many are wounded.

Violence is on the increase. Some of your people want to retaliate. You are no longer able to control their violent acts of retaliation and counter-retaliation.

Your leadership team comes to the sobering realization that you will never achieve what you desire unless you break away from the mother country and create a new nation – a whole new country!

Assignment

Declare independence from the mother country and begin the process of creating a new country. **(Please see note on page 55.)**

- ❑ **Day 1** – Write your Declaration of Independence (page 19-21).
- ❑ **Day 2** – Make a map of your new country (see page 22).

Retaliation

It was May of 1775. The British had captured the weapons and ammunition stockpiled in Concord. The Patriot fighters had come up with a daring plan: capture the British fort, Ticonderoga, in New York. Who would lead such a dangerous mission? Enter: Ethan Allen and his Green Mountain Boys.

Ethan had settled in the Green Mountain area. The colony of New Hampshire had sold this land to Ethan and other farm settlers. King George, however, said that New Hampshire couldn't sell the land – because it belonged to New York. Now New York wanted the farmers to pay for the same land they had already purchased from New Hampshire! Ethan and his Green Mountain Boys had spent years fighting the New Yorkers who tried to move onto their land, giving them plenty of experience fighting in the wilderness. Now the Patriots wanted Ethan and his men to capture the fort.

Ethan sent a spy to the Fort to discover the number of soldiers and its weaknesses. With this information, he was able to capture the fort, its cannons, and its weapons for the Patriots. What did Ethan yell as he entered the Fort? "In the name of the great Jehovah and the Continental Congress!"

Lesson 9

How Did They Decide?

It was May of 1775, a month after the Revolutionary War began. Delegates from all 13 colonies met in Philadelphia to decide what course of action they should take next. In His sovereignty, God designed it that the greatest minds in America were assembled together. They worked for more than a year. Here are a few of the incredible decisions they made:
- They adopted the various patriot militias to form a single American army. George Washington was elected to lead it.
- They established a postal system for communications. Ben Franklin was elected to lead it.
- After nearly a year, the colonies were convinced that they could not settle their differences. *They declared themselves a free and independent nation.* The Declaration of Independence was signed July 4, 1776.

This final act was an act of treason, promising a death sentence to anyone brave enough to sign it. Fifty-six men signed it.

Your declaration of independence has caused your mother country to declare war on you. It is indeed a sobering thing to be at war with a great world power. Your own supporters are divided now. Some are 100% behind you, but others are not so sure. Although they wanted change and the political power necessary to make those changes, they never intended to establish a whole new country – and they certainly hadn't anticipated a war!

Assignment

You must bring unity to your supporters and convince those who are wavering that the establishment of a new country is essential – no matter what the cost.

❑ **Day 1** – Create a flag (page 25)
❑ **Day 2** – Bring unity to your supporters (page 26)

Our New Flag

The colors and emblems on a flag aren't just pretty to look at. They are always symbolic of something. Let's look at the flag of the United States for example. The flag has thirteen stripes, alternating red and white. These represent the thirteen original colonies. The red is to remind us of valor and hardiness. The white represents purity. The US flag also has 50 stars on a field of blue. The stars, as you know, represent the 50 states, and the color blue signifies vigilance, perseverance, and justice.

In the box below, create and color your new country's flag. On the lines beneath it, explain the significance of your chosen colors and emblems.

My Flag

_____
_____
_____
_____
_____
_____
_____

Laying Out The Plan

26

You have called a congress of great men to bring unity to your organization and to consolidate your political powers. Yours is an awesome task. Use the worksheet below to accomplish the task. (**Please see note on page 55.**)

1. Your people must be reminded that the creation of this new nation is God's will. After all, if God is not behind this endeavor, it is sure to fail. Write a paragraph demonstrating how this new nation is God's will (using Scripture would help): _____
_____
_____

2. Write a paragraph demonstrating how your new nation will benefit future generations of its citizens. What blessings and freedoms will they enjoy that you did not enjoy? _____
_____
_____
_____

3. To insure that the government of your new nation runs smoothly, you must see to it that certain offices remain in place. Explain how you will reform, organize, and utilize each of the following in your new government. Keep in mind that the remnants of many of these are already in place – leftovers from the mother country. Remember to think strategically. You are trying to win your freedom *and* the support of your people! Use these assets wisely!:

- Turnpikes and roads: _____
_____

- Postal system/stamps: _____
_____

- Education system: _____
_____

- National security and defense: _____
_____

- Power supplies: _____
_____

- Environment protection: _____
_____

- National parks and monuments: _____
_____

- Telecommunications and Internet: _____
_____

Teacher's Note: Please read over the assignments your student did on page 25 and 26. If your student effectively won the support of his people, proceed to lesson 10 on page 27. If your student failed to gain the support of his people, proceed to lesson 11 on page 29.

Lesson 10

Thankfully, you have won the support of your people. Your new country has been born in the midst of war. Your newly-won unity infuses new purpose and hope into the cause, and you face the war with a will to win. However, you are pitted against a much larger power. It's going to take more than just a *will* to win.

Assignment

You must convince your neighboring countries and/or states to join you as your allies. You must convince them that friendship with your country will benefit them in the end.

Being On The Losing Side

What do you do when you are losing battle after battle (with only a few victories to enjoy) in a war against a superpower? Here's what General Washington did during the winter of 1777-78.

The British were camped comfortably in Philadelphia for the winter. They had plenty of food and shelter and even the pleasure of society. The Continental army, however, was camped nearly 20 miles away in Valley Forge. They had little food or shelter, and, in many cases, little clothing and no shoes! It was a severe winter, and things looked hopeless. Morale was very low.

General Washington and the Prussian drillmaster, Baron Von Steuben, began working with the soldiers. They drilled them with military precision daily, soldier by soldier. Washington prayed for them daily. No battles were fought that winter.

By spring, the men had turned from a ragtag band of undisciplined fighters into a lean, mean, fighting machine – and as a result, the tide of the war began to turn.

Allied Forces

You will be using this worksheet to draft alliances with neighboring countries and/or states. As you work on your alliances, keep in mind that often they form naturally with those who are religiously and philosophically like-minded. Also, think of your assets. What can you offer your allies to offset the sacrifices they will make in your behalf? **(Please see note on page 56.)**

1. Which countries would you like to approach in order to form an alliance (also consider geography – your closest neighbors)? Why did you choose these countries? What will each be able to offer?

   _____
   _____
   _____

2. List the benefits they will enjoy by allying with you. What will you be able to do for them in the following areas:

- Religiously and philosophically: _____
   _____
   _____

- Politically: _____
   _____
   _____
   _____

- Economically: _____
   _____
   _____
   _____

- Technologically: _____
   _____
   _____
   _____

Write a paragraph declaring your commitment to your allies: _____
   _____
   _____
   _____

Teacher's Note: Please read over the assignment your student did on this page. If your student effectively won the support of his allies, proceed to lesson 12 on page 30. If your student failed to gain the support of his allies, proceed to lesson 13 on page 31.

Lesson 11

You have been unable to win the support of your people. Your new country is divided and strife-torn. The population is in despair. An even larger problem looms. You are pitted against a much larger power. As a divided nation, your new country has little hope of winning its independence.

Assignment

You must convince your neighboring countries and/or states to join you as your allies. It is your only remaining option. You must convince them that friendship with your country will benefit them in the end.

❏ Do the assignment on page 28.

Convincing Allies

It was the fall of 1777. The Patriots weren't getting the help they desired from other countries. After all, no one wants to join the war on the losing side! And now the British General, Burgoyne, decided to stop the Americans once and for all. He and his men head for Saratoga, New York. An amazing thing happened, however. All along Burgoyne's route, snipers picked off his men one by one. Farmers from the surrounding area headed for the Continental army to lend their support. The American army grew and grew until it was three times bigger than the British army.

On October 17, 1777, the American army defeated the British at Saratoga. But that wasn't all. General Burgoyne surrendered his entire army to the Americans! They were made to swear an oath not to fight against Americans any longer, then put on ships and sent back to England!

When the French heard of this victory, do you think they were more willing to join the Americans in the battle for independence? Yes, they were!

Lesson 12

Did You Know…

- The United States did not have *the* Constitution until 8 years after the war…

- The law of the land during this time period was called "The Articles of Confederation"…

- During those 8 years, each state had more power than the central government…

- John Hanson served as the first president of the new country…

- There were 7 more presidents after him during that 8-year period…

- Several states at first refused to ratify the new Constitution, because it didn't guarantee personal rights…

- The new Constitution was amended 3 years later with the addition of the Bill of Rights…

- George Washington became the 9th president of the United States, but the first one to be *elected by the people* under the new Constitution.

Congratulations! With the help of your allies, you have won the revolution! You have won your independence, and your new nation is now a reality.

It is a heavy burden you bear – to birth a nation unlike any other. It is up to you and your leaders to guarantee freedom to your citizens for generations to come. Was the loss of lives and the devastation worth it? You must make it so.

Assignment

You will need a Constitution to govern your country. You will need a ruler. You will need money.

- ❑ **Day 1** – Read the outline of the Constitution (page 32-33), then establish the foundational principles of your constitution (page 34).
- ❑ **Day 2** – Expand the principles of your constitution. (Page 35)
- ❑ **Day 3** – Write the final copy of your constitution and ratify it (page 36). **(Please see note on page 56.)**
- ❑ **Day 4** - Place your leader in power. **(Please see note on page 56.)**
- ❑ **Day 5** – Create a money and tax systems.
- ❑ **Day 6** – Rebuild your war-torn nation.

Lesson 13

Our Condolences to you over the heavy losses you suffered in your attempted revolution. You have lost your bid for independence and your dreams have evaporated like smoke.

It is a heavy burden you bear as you see the loss of lives and the devastation around you, yet one good thing has arisen. Your revolution has awakened the conscience of the people of your mother country.

It is up to you and your leaders to lead the way in this reawakening – to guarantee freedom to the citizens for generations to come.

> "We have staked the whole future of America upon the capacity of each…of us to govern ourselves…according to the Ten Commandments."
> James Madison

> "…the smiles of Heaven can never be expected on a nation that disregards the eternal rules of order and right…"
> George Washington
> In his inaugural address of 1789

Assignment

You will need to hold a constitutional convention. You will need a new president. You will need to rebuild the fractured nation.

- ❏ **Day 1** – Read the outline of the Constitution (page 32-33), then establish the foundational principles of your constitution (page 34).
- ❏ **Day 2** – Expand the principles of your constitution (page 35).
- ❏ **Day 3** – Write the final copy of your constitution and ratify it (page 36). **(Please see note on page 56.)**.
- ❏ **Day 4** – Place your leader in power. **(Please see note on page 56.)**
- ❏ **Day 5** – Reorganize your money and tax systems.
- ❏ **Day 6** – Rebuild your war-torn nation.

> "No people can be [required] to acknowledge and adore the Invisible Hand which conducts the affairs of men more than the people of the United States. Every step by which they have [become] an independent nation seems to have been distinguished by some token of Providential agency."
> George Washington
> In his inaugural address of 1789

> "…the religion which has introduced civil liberty is the religion of Christ and His apostles."
> Noah Webster

The Constitution of the United States – Briefly Paraphrased and Outlined

We, the people of the United States, for the purpose of forming a more perfect union, do the following:
- Establish a justice system
- Insure peace within our borders
- Provide national security
- Promote the welfare of all
- Secure the blessings of liberty to ourselves and our children's children.

To accomplish this we conduct and establish this Constitution of the United States of America.

Article 1

Section 1

All legislative powers that are given in this document shall be placed in a congress. This congress will consist of a **Senate** and a **House of Representatives**.

Section 2

Representatives will be chosen every two years by the people of each state. The representative must be at least 25 years old, a citizen for at least 7 years, and he must live in the state he represents. The number of representatives is to be determined by population.

Representatives have the sole power of impeachment.

Section 3

There will be two senators from each state, chosen by the state's legislature, who will serve six years. A senator must be at least 30 years old, be a citizen for at least 9 years, and he must live in the state he represents.

The vice president of the United States is also the president of the senate. Senators have the sole power to try impeachment, and to remove those impeached from office.

Section 4

Each state will be in charge of its own elections for its congressmen, but Congress may regulate these elections. Congress must meet at least once each year.

Section 5

Each house determines its own rules of conducting its meetings, and may do business if they have a majority present. Each house must keep a public journal of its meetings – unless it concerns something top-secret.

Section 6

Congressmen will be paid. They are exempt from arrest unless it is for treason, a felony, or a breach of peace. Congressmen can only hold one government office at a time.

Section 7

Tax bills start in the House of Representatives. All bills must be signed by the president before they become law. If he vetoes it, both houses may override his veto with a 2/3-majority vote.

Section 8

Congress handles all taxes necessary to run the government. They have the power to borrow money. They can regulate trade and commerce. They may determine the laws concerning bankruptcy. They will coin money. They will make the laws necessary to prevent counterfeiting. They will establish a postal system. They will make copyright laws to protect invention, art, and discovery. They have the power to punish piracy. They have the power to declare war. They have the power to raise and support an army. They have the power to provide and maintain a navy. They have the power to designate a national capital and to oversee the building of forts, arsenals, and other necessary buildings. They have the power to make any laws necessary to carry out the above duties.

Section 9

Congress will regulate immigration. Citizens are protected against being arrested without reason. If there is no reason for the arrest, the citizen is to be immediately set free. If a person has done something, it is illegal to make a law against that action and punish that person after the fact. There will not be a head tax. There will be no taxes on state-to-state exports or imports. No state will be treated preferentially. Any government money that is used must be accounted for. No titles of nobility will be recognized.

Section 10

Anything written about in the preceding sections are the rights and duties of the national government and the individual states do not have the power to do any of the above.

(Continued, next page...)

Article 2
Section 1

A president and a vice president will be elected to a 4-year term. Each state appoints electors equal to the number of senators and representatives. The president is chosen by the electors. Only natural-born citizens can be president, and must be at least 35 years old, and have lived here for at least 14 years. If the president is removed from office for any reason, the vice president will fill his place. The president will get paid, but he will not get a raise during his time in office. He must take an oath of allegiance to uphold the Constitution while in office.

Section 2

The president will serve as the commander-in-chief of the military. He can make treaties, appoint ambassadors and justices, etc. These must be approved by a 2/3-majority vote in congress. He may appoint people to fill vacancies.

Section 3

The president must give a state-of-the-union address, receive foreign leaders, and make sure that the laws are faithfully executed.

Section 4

The president and the vice president can be impeached for treason, bribery, high crimes, and misdemeanors.

Article 3
Section 1

A Supreme Court and inferior courts will be established. Judges hold office for life (assuming good behavior), and will receive a salary.

Section 2

The Supreme Court will rule over cases involving states and cases involving ambassadors and diplomats. Everyone is guaranteed a trial by jury in the state where the crime was committed.

Section 3

Treason is considered to be making war against this government or helping the enemy. There must be two witnesses for someone to be convicted of treason, or a confession. Congress has the power to punish treason.

Article 4
Section 1

Each state must respect the laws of every other state. Congress may regulate these laws.

Section 2

The citizens of every state have the same privileges as stated in this Constitution. If a person commits a crime, he will be sent back to the state where the crime was committed. If you are bound to serve, you can't escape by running away.

Section 3

New states can join the union, but not within the boundaries of the already-established states. Congress is in charge of all territories and United States property.

Section 4

Every state in the union is guaranteed a republican form of government and protection against invasion and violence.

Article 5
This Constitution can be amended if 2/3 of both houses propose it and ¾ of the states ratify it.

Article 6
The United States will honor its debts. The Constitution and any treaties made under it are the supreme law of the land. Although those serving in these positions are bound by an oath, it is not based on a particular religion.

Article 7
When nine states ratify this Constitution, it will be the supreme law of the land.

Ratified September 17, 1787

Getting the Basics

1. The preamble to the Constitution is a brief introduction outlining the main objectives of the Constitution. Referring to the example preamble on page 32, create the preamble to your constitution: _____
   _____
   _____
   _____

2. The United States government has three branches (executive, judicial, and legislative) to provide a balance of powers. How many branches will your government have? _____

3. **Article 1:** If you have a legislative branch, how many houses will it have?(The US has two, the House of Representatives and the Senate.) ____ What are the names of your houses? _____
   _____
   The US Senate allows 2 senators per state, regardless of population. The US House of Representatives allows a number of representatives based on the population of the state. How will you determine the number of representatives in your new government? _____
   _____
   _____

4. **Article 2:** If you have an executive branch, what will your executive title be (president, king, shah, emperor, czar, etc.)? _____

5. **Article 3:** If you have a judicial branch, what will you call it? (The judicial branch of the United States is the Supreme Court.)_____
   How many justices will it have? (The United States has 9.) _____

6. **Article 4** of the Constitution is about the duties of each individual state (see Article 4 on page 33 for reference). Does your new nation have states? _____ If so, what are they called (states, territories, provinces, etc.)? _____ How many do you have? _____ What duties do they have? _____
   _____

7. How do you go about changing your constitution if necessary? (See **Article 5** on page 33 for reference.) _____
   _____

8. Establish your constitution as the supreme law of your land (see **Article 6** on page 33 for reference). _____
   _____
   _____

34

Refining It

1. Referring to the work you did on **page 34**, expand **Article 1** of your constitution. What qualifications are needed for this job? What are his duties? Study **Article 1** on **page 32** for ideas. _____
   _____
   _____
   _____
   _____

2. Now, expand your **Article 2** (see **page 34**). What are the qualifications for this job? What are the duties inherent in this job? Refer to the outline of **Article 2** on **page 33** for ideas. _____
   _____
   _____
   _____
   _____

3. Next, expand your **Article 3** (see **page 34**). What are the qualifications for this job? What are the duties? Refer to **Article 3** on **page 33** for ideas.
   _____
   _____
   _____
   _____
   _____

4. Do you want to have additional branches in your government? If so, describe the qualifications and duties of those branches here:
   _____
   _____
   _____

5. Do you want to add any additional articles to your constitution that are not covered in the US Constitution? If so, add them here: _____
   _____
   _____
   _____
   _____

Tomorrow you will combine the work you did on pages 34 and 35 to create the final copy of your constitution.

Constitution

Done in convention by the unanimous consent of those present on the date of

Vote Smart!

This assignment will help you to create your candidate for leading your new nation. (**See note on page 56.**)

Your candidate's name:
_____

Age: _____

Describe your candidate's family (Is he/she married with children?):
_____
_____
_____

> In this box you will paste a picture of your candidate. Look through magazines to find a picture that represents the way your candidate looks. Keep in mind that appearance is, unfortunately, important to many people. A candidate that appears slovenly, play-boyish, or ignorant, even if he is very organized, capable, and intelligent, will have a hard time overcoming his outward appearance in the eyes of an appearance-worshipping society. Choose the appearance of your candidate carefully.
>
> "For the LORD sees not as man sees: man looks on the outward appearance, but the LORD looks on the heart."
> 1 Samuel 16:7B ESV

Describe your candidate's education and job experience that qualify him for the job:
_____
_____
_____
_____
_____

Create a campaign button in the circle above.

How will your candidate rebuild this war-torn nation if he wins the election? What is his philosophy?
_____
_____
_____
_____
_____
_____
_____
_____
_____

Render to Caesar…

- Today you will begin coining money. Looking at the map of your nation (page 21), where is your mint located? _____

- The main currency of the United States is the dollar. Coins represent fractions of a dollar. The smallest denomination is the penny, which is 1/100th of a dollar. The motto, "In God we trust," appears on all United States currency. What is the main currency of your nation called? _____ What is the smallest denomination and what is it worth? _____ Do you have a national motto, and will it appear on your money? If so, what is it? _____

- In the boxes below, design the front and back of your main currency, as well as the front and back of your smallest-denomination coin:

Front

Front

Back

Back

Continue on to the next page………………………………………………………

Render to Caesar…..(cont.)

1. You will need to collect taxes in order to run your government. Explain your tax system: How do you levy taxes? How much? How often do your citizens have to pay? _____
   _____
   _____
   _____

2. Will you collect Federal taxes? Yes or no
   Will you collect state taxes? Yes or no
   Will you collect local taxes? Yes or no
   Will you collect sales taxes? Yes or no If yes, how much? _____
   Will you collect social security? Yes or no

3. Who must pay taxes in your new nation? Who is exempt? _____
   _____
   _____
   _____

4. What will you do for the new nation with the taxes you collect? _____
   _____
   _____
   _____

5. What will the taxes you collect *not* be used for? _____
   _____
   _____
   _____

6. What will be the punishment be for citizens who don't pay their taxes? ___
   _____
   _____
   _____

Note: The information on this page will later be used to amend your constitution.

Rebuilding a War-Torn Nation

1. The Bible says in Psalm 34:14 that we should "Seek peace and pursue it." Describe the treaty you will make with the mother country to insure peace.

   _____
   _____
   _____
   _____
   _____
   _____

2. Your country saw many lives lost. You now have many widows and orphans in the land. What, if anything will your government do for the families of your nation's fallen heroes? _____
   _____
   _____
   _____

3. In the box to the right, design a monument to honor those who died fighting for the nation:

4. To rebuild your economy, you will want to establish trade with the mother country. How will you convince the citizens of that country that re-establishing trade will benefit them?

   _____
   _____
   _____
   _____

5. Your soldiers are returning to their homes and jobs. Factories will no longer need to build military equipment. What steps will you take to create jobs for your homebound soldiers and to rebuild your economy? _____
   _____
   _____
   _____
   _____

Lesson 14

The citizens of your new nation have worked hard to establish your new nation. The economy is growing and robust. You have established yourself among the great nations of the world.

However, there seems to be a growing unrest among your people. Cases have arisen that are testing your new constitution.

Assignment

You will be designing a bill of rights to amend your constitution. (**See note on page 56-57**.)

- **Day 1** – Read Amendment 1 of the paraphrased Bill of Rights on page 42. Do the assignment on page 44.
- **Day 2** – Read Amendments 2-6 of the paraphrased Bill of Rights on page 42. Do the assignment on page 45.
- **Day 3** – Read Amendments 7-11 of the paraphrased Bill of Rights on page 42. Do the assignment on page 46.
- **Day 4** – Read Amendments 12-16 of the paraphrased Bill of Rights on pages 42-43. Do the assignment on page 47
- **Day 5** – Read Amendments 17-22 of the paraphrased Bill of Rights on page 43. Do the assignment on page 48.
- **Day 6** – Read Amendments 23-27 of the paraphrased Bill of Rights on page 43. Do the assignment on page 49.
- **Day 7** – Write the final draft of your constitutional amendments on page 50-52. You will need pages 44-49 to complete this assignment.

Congratulations! You have finished!

It Wasn't Good Enough?

The Constitution was adopted in 1787. Many people weren't happy with the constitution because it didn't have a bill of rights. It was conceivable that the rights of the people could erode over time if those rights weren't protected. The Bill of Rights (the first ten amendments) was added to the Constitution and ratified in 1791. The Bill of Rights protects our most basic rights, like freedom of religion and speech.

Amendments to the Constitution of the United States
Briefly Paraphrased and Outlined
(The first ten amendments are known as **The Bill of Rights**)

The 1st Amendment
Congress is not allowed to make laws that would establish a particular religion, prohibit free speech or free press, prohibit peaceful assemblies of people, or prohibit people from appealing to the government to correct any wrongs it has done.

The 2nd Amendment
Because a well-armed militia is necessary to state security, congress may not make laws that infringe on the right of the people to keep and bear arms.

The 3rd Amendment
In peacetime, citizens will no longer be forced to house soldiers without their consent. During war, citizens may be required to house soldiers, but only in a manner legalized by congress.

The 4th Amendment
Citizens have the right to be secure in their persons, their houses, their papers and personal property. A search and seizure warrant can be issued only if it is legally authorized and there is a good reason for it. The warrant must describe the particular person/place/thing to be searched or seized.

The 5th Amendment
Citizens cannot be tried for a serious crime unless a grand jury formally charges them first. A person can't be tried twice for the same crime. A person can't be forced to testify against himself. The government can't take a person's life, liberty, or property without due process of the law. Private property cannot be taken for public use unless the owner is paid fairly for it.

The 6th Amendment
In criminal cases, a citizen has the right to a speedy and public trial by an impartial jury, in the state/district where the crime was committed. He has the right to know the crime of which he is being charged. He has the right to confront his accusers. He has the right to compel witnesses in his favor to testify for him, and he has the right to have a lawyer to defend him.

The 7th Amendment
In lawsuits, a citizen has the right to a trial by jury to decide the issue.

The 8th Amendment
Excessive bail and excessive fines are prohibited. So is cruel and unusual punishment.

The 9th Amendment
Listing these rights in this constitution does not deny or downplay other rights our citizens have that aren't listed here.

The 10th Amendment
Any power that is not given to the new nation by this constitution, or any power that is not taken away from the states or the people, are given to the states and the people.

The 11th Amendment
A citizen of any nation cannot sue a state in a federal court.

The 12th Amendment
Electors in each state will vote for and make lists of presidential and vice-presidential candidates. These lists will be sent, sealed, to the president of the senate. The lists will be opened and totaled in the presence of both houses. The presidential and vice-presidential candidates with the greatest number of votes will be president. If no one has the majority, the House of Representatives will elect the president from a list of 3 candidates, and the senate will elect the vice-president from a list of 2 candidates. The House has until March 4 to elect a president, or the vice-president will become acting president. If a person is not eligible to be president, then he is not eligible to be vice-president either.

The 13th Amendment
There will be no slavery in this nation, except as punishment for a crime.

The 14th Amendment
- If you were born in this country, you are a citizen of this country and your state. No laws can be made to take away your rights. States cannot take away your life, liberty, or property without a legal process.
- All male, tax-paying citizens who are 21 and older may vote. The number of representatives in each state will be determined by the state's population. If a state prevents its citizens from voting, it will lose representation in congress.
- If you ever took part in a rebellion against the nation, you cannot hold a public office.
- The country will honor all its debts except debts that were created because of rebellion against this country, or debts created by freeing slaves.

Amendments to the Constitution of the United States
Briefly Paraphrased and Outlined – Continued

The 15th Amendment
All citizens can vote, regardless of race.

The 16th Amendment
Congress has the power to collect tax on a citizen's income, no matter how he makes his money. The amount will not be equally divided among the states or the people.

The 17th Amendment
Senators will be elected by the people, 2 from each state, for a 6-year term. Each senator gets one vote in congress. If a vacancy happens in the senate, that state's governor will hold a special election to fill the vacancy. The governor can appoint a temporary replacement.

The 18th Amendment
One year after this amendment is ratified, it will be illegal to make, sell, or transport alcoholic beverages in this country. The power to enforce this law will be shared by federal and state government.

The 19th Amendment
Women have the right to vote.

The 20th Amendment
- The terms of the president and vice-president end on January 20. The terms of senators and representatives end on January 3. The terms of their successors begin those same days.
- Congress will meet at least once a year, beginning January 3.
- If the president-elect dies before taking office, the vice-president-elect becomes president. If a president hasn't been chosen by January 20 or doesn't qualify, then the vice-president-elect will fill in until one is chosen. Congress can choose a temporary president until a president or vice-president is elected.
- If the House of Representatives has chosen a president, or the senate a vice-president, and he dies before taking office, the House or Senate can make a law to decide what to do.

The 21st Amendment
The 18th Amendment is repealed on the federal level. Each state can make its laws regarding prohibition, and these state laws will be recognized by the federal government.

The 22nd Amendment
A person can only be elected to serve as president for two terms (8 years), plus no more than 2 years of someone else's term, for a total of no more than 10 years.

The 23rd Amendment
The citizens of Washington DC are allowed to have the same number of presidential electors as the state with the lowest population.

The 24th Amendment
Failure to pay a poll tax will not prevent a citizen from voting in national elections.

The 25th Amendment
- If the president is removed from office, the vice-president becomes president.
- If the vice-president is removed from office, the president will nominate a vice-president. This nominee must then be confirmed by a majority vote in both houses of congress.
- When the president writes to both houses that he can no longer serve as president (such as due to illness), the vice-president becomes president.
- When the vice-president and a majority of the presidential cabinet believe the president is unable to serve as president, they must write to both houses. At that time, the vice-president immediately becomes president. When the president feels he is recovered, he must write to both houses. If the vice-president disagrees, he must get a majority vote from both houses to agree with him. Congress then has 21 days to decide the issue, requiring a 2/3 majority in both houses to keep the president from returning to office.

The 26th Amendment
A citizen can vote when he turns 18 years old.

The 27th Amendment
Pay raises for congressmen will not take effect until after elections.

It's Only Right – Day 1

44

You will be amending your constitution to further strengthen the cause of liberty in your new nation. To complete this exercise, you will need the constitution you wrote on page 36 and the paraphrase of the constitutional amendments on pages 42- 43. *Please refer to the first amendment for this exercise.*
You will be creating the first amendment of your constitution. <u>See note on page 57.</u>

1. All the Christian churches in your nation want to reinstate prayer, Bible reading, and recognition of the Ten Commandments in public schools. In opposition, the Muslims are demanding equal access. They want daily prayer to Allah for the students as well as Koran reading. Does your current constitution deal with issues of religion? If so, how? If not, you will need to amend your constitution: _____
_____
_____

2. Some Christians have set up a counseling booth in front of an abortion clinic to counsel potential patients against having abortions. The clinic owners sue the Christians to keep them from talking to their patients. At the same time, abortion clinics have been setting up offices in the public schools to provide counseling to the students. The Christians are trying to stop them. Does your constitution deal with issues of free speech? If so, how? If not, you will need to amend your constitution: _____
_____
_____

3. A group of homosexuals are trying to have books that support homosexuality printed and placed in the public schools. Christians are trying to get creation textbooks placed in public schools. Both groups are trying to stop the other. Does your current constitution deal with issues of the press and censorship? If so, how? If not, you will need to amend your constitution: _____
_____
_____

4. A group of Christians is promoting a large gathering (1,000 people are expected) to discuss why homosexuality is both sinful and detrimental, and how to stop the homosexual agenda. The homosexuals want the police to stop them because they claim the Christians are supporting discrimination. At the same time, the homosexuals are hosting a large, peaceful gathering to educate people and promote their agenda. Does your current constitution deal with peaceful assembly? If so, how? If not, you will need to amend your constitution: _____
_____
_____

5. During your revolution, your military accidentally dropped a bomb in a residential area, destroying a house in your own nation. The owners are now suing your government to have their property restored. Does your current constitution deal with grievances the people may have against the government? If so, how? If not, you will need to amend your constitution: _____
_____
_____

It's Only Right – Day 2

You will be amending your constitution to further strengthen the cause of liberty in your new nation. To complete this exercise, you will need the constitution you wrote on page 36 and the paraphrase of the constitutional amendments on pages 42- 43. *Please refer to the 2nd-6th amendments for this exercise.*

You will be creating the 2nd- 6th amendments of your constitution. <u>See note on page 57.</u>

1. There is a neo-nazi gang in town. They have been stockpiling automatic weapons. Crime is on the rise. Citizens can't walk through the city without fear of being mugged. Refer to the 2nd amendment on page 42 and the constitution you wrote on page 36. Does your constitution deal with armed citizens? If so, how? If not, you will need to amend your constitution: _____
_____
_____

2. The war is over, but the militia is still on duty patrolling the border. As there are no barracks yet to house the soldiers, you consider billeting them with area families. Refer to the 3rd amendment on page 42, and the constitution you wrote on page 36. Does your current constitution deal with the housing of soldiers? If so, how? If not, you will need to amend your constitution: _____
_____

3. You receive a tip at government headquarters that terrorists are headquartered in the center of a residential neighborhood. According to the tip, the terrorists fear detection and will be moving to new location as soon as possible. You drive by the lovely home in the quiet neighborhood. Neighbors on either side of the suspected location swear that it isn't a terrorist hideout, but a respectable young family with four children living there. You need to get in there to discover the truth before it's too late. Please refer to page 36 and to the 4th amendment on page 42. Does your current constitution deal with issues of search and seizure? If so, how? If not, you will need to amend your constitution:_____
_____
_____

4. A major battle of the war took place in Farmer Scott's cornfield. You would like to turn the acreage into a national cemetery and monument for those who died there. Please refer to page 36 and to the 5th amendment on page 42. Does your current constitution deal with issues of public and private property? If so, how? If not, you will need to amend your constitution: _____
_____

5. The citizens in Jeantown are fed up with the local thugs. Since the law can't seem to control them, the townspeople take matters into their own hands. Late one night, they break into the homes of the thugs, cuff them, and drag them to the center of town for punishment. Please refer to page 36 and to the 6th amendment on page 42. Does your current constitution deal with issues of criminal justice? If so, how? If not, you will need to amend your constitution: _____
_____
_____

It's Only Right – Day 3

46

You will be amending your constitution to further strengthen the cause of liberty in your new nation. To complete this exercise, you will need the constitution you wrote on page 36 and the paraphrase of the constitutional amendments on pages 42- 43. *Please refer to the 7th-11th amendments for this exercise.*

You will be creating the 7th-11th amendments of your constitution. See note on page 57.

1. Portal Jones and Fenster Smith are arguing about who must pay for the damages to Portal's car. The car was damaged when a tree fell on it. Portal claims that the tree, which was on Fenster's property, was dead and that Fenster knew it was in danger of falling. Fenster claims he had an appointment scheduled with a tree-removal service. He claims he told Portal of the appointment and warned him of an upcoming storm; but Portal insisted on parking his car next to the dead tree anyway. Portal claims Fenster never warned him of the storm or told him of the appointment. Please refer to your constitution on page 36 and the 7th amendment on page 42. Does your constitution deal with lawsuits? If so, how? If not, you will need to amend your constitution now: _____

2. The citizens from Jeanstown have placed all the town's thugs in stocks. They have been throwing rotten food and filth at them. Each thug has received 40 lashes. The townspeople were filming the event to show in the public schools as a warning to any would-be thugs. Please refer to page 36 and to the 8th amendment on page 42. Does your current constitution deal with issues of criminal punishment? If so, how? If not, you will need to amend your constitution: _____

3. Karen Shair wants to have her baby in the privacy of her own home with a midwife, but she heard that it's illegal. She believes she has the right to do this, even if it isn't specifically mentioned in the constitution. Please refer to page 36 and to the 9th amendment on page 42. Does your current constitution deal with other rights? If so, how? If not, you will need to amend your constitution now: _____

4. An abortionist has set up a clinic in town. He claims that the right to have an abortion is a state issue rather than a federal issue. Please refer to page 36 and the 10th amendment on page 42. Does your current constitution deal with issues of states' rights? If so, how? If not, you will need to amend your constitution now: _____

5. Burl Lee Mann, who lives in the mother country, is suing one of your states. His business happens to be located across the border in the new nation, and as a result, he is bankrupt – the war prevented him from crossing the border. Please refer to page 36 and the 11th amendment on page 42. Does your current constitution deal with state lawsuits? If so, how? If not, you will need to amend your constitution: _____

It's Only Right – Day 4

You will be amending your constitution to further strengthen the cause of liberty in your new nation. To complete this exercise, you will need the constitution you wrote on page 36 and the paraphrase of the constitutional amendments on pages 42- 43. *Please refer to the 12th-16th amendments for this exercise.*

You will be creating the 12th- 16th amendments of your constitution. <u>See note on page 58.</u>

1. It is election time again. Your first elections had some glitches in them. Please refer to page 36, and to the 12th amendment on page 42. Does your current constitution deal with issues of election? If so, how? If not, you will need to amend your constitution now: _____
_____
_____

2. Farmer Liverwurst, who lives on the border, reportedly has been catching illegal immigrants who are trying to sneak across the border into the country. Apparently he has been offering them a deal: Work my fields, and I won't turn you in. I'll let you sleep in the barn and give you two meals a day. If you don't comply, I'll turn you over to immigration services. Refer to page 36, and to the 13th amendment on page 42. Does your current constitution deal with issues of slavery? If so, how? If not, you will need to amend your constitution: _____
_____

3. Simon Cez is running for governor. During the revolution, he had actively campaigned against the leaders and agenda of your revolutionaries. He had managed to get several of your leaders jailed, and even wrote a best-selling book "exposing" your organization. But, now that the revolution is over and your new nation is established, Mr. Cez seems to have changed his mind and would like to be a governor in the new nation. Refer to page 36, and to the 14th amendment on page 42. Does your current constitution deal with rebels? If so, how? If not, You will need to amend your constitution: _____
_____

4. Erna Buck lives in the new nation – but not by choice! Her home just happens to be on that side of the border! She, however, considers herself to be a true Mother-Countrian. She was born and raised there! On election day, she is turned away at the polls, since she is a Mother-Countrian. Refer to page 36, and to the 15th amendment on page 43. Does your current constitution deal with issues of race and voting? If so, how? If not, you will need to amend your constitution: _____
_____

5. There is concern that the new nation is nearly bankrupt. You still have a huge military to maintain, as well as widows and orphans to support. There are employees that need to be paid, as well as postal services to maintain. The list goes on and on. You need money. Refer to page 36 and page 39, and to the 16th amendment on page 43. You will need to craft a tax amendment for your constitution based on the information you've written on those pages: _____
_____
_____

It's Only Right – Day 5

You will be amending your constitution to further strengthen the cause of liberty in your new nation. To complete this exercise, you will need the constitution you wrote on page 36 and the paraphrase of the constitutional amendments on pages 42- 43. *Please refer to the 17th-22nd amendments for this exercise.*
You will be creating the 17th- 21st amendments of your constitution. See note on page 58.

1. Senator Morgantropple has died. The people of his state are upset, because they are not equally represented in congress. Please refer to page 36, and to the 17th amendments on page 43. Does your current constitution deal with senatorial vacancies? If so, how? If not, you will need to amend your constitution: _____
   _____
   _____

2. Drunken parties seem to be the new national craze. Kids are drinking at earlier and earlier ages. Accidents involving drunk drivers are on the rise. So is spouse and child abuse. Alcohol sales have skyrocketed. Refer to page 36, and to both the 18th and 21st amendments on page 43. Does your current constitution deal with issues of alcohol? If so, how? If not, you may wish to amend your constitution: _____
   _____
   _____

3. Erna Buck has once more appeared at the polls on election day. She is turned away again – this time, because she is a woman. Refer to page 36, and to the 19th amendment on page 43. Does your current constitution deal with issues of women voting? If so, how? If not, you will need to amend your constitution: _____
   _____
   _____

4. Election day is finally over. The people have chosen Frank N. Stine as their new president and Drake U. Law as Vice President. President-elect Stine is suddenly stricken with a fatal heart attack just two days before taking office. Refer to page 36, and to the 20th amendment on page 43. Does your current constitution deal with the death of a president or vice-president elect? If so, how? If not, you will need to amend your constitution: _____
   _____
   _____

5. Drake U. Law ends up being a very popular president. The people elect him over and over again. Ten years. Twenty years. Thirty years go by, and President Law is still in office. Refer to page 36, and to the 22nd amendment on page 43. Does your current constitution deal with presidential term limits? If so, how? If not, you may want to amend your constitution: _____
   _____
   _____

It's Only Right – Day 6

You will be amending your constitution to further strengthen the cause of liberty in your new nation. To complete this exercise, you will need the constitution you wrote on page 36 and the paraphrase of the constitutional amendments on pages 42- 43. *Please refer to the 23rd-27th amendments for this exercise.*
You will be creating the final amendments of your constitution. See note on page 58.

1. The citizens in your national capital are really upset. Since they don't technically belong to any state, they haven't been able to vote in presidential elections. They are staging demonstrations because they haven't been represented in congress. Refer to page 36, and to the 23rd amendment on page 43. Does your current constitution deal with the issue of representation for the citizens of the capital? If so, how? If not, you will need to amend your constitution: _____
_____
_____

2. At the election poll in Boredville, election officials have been charging a poll tax of $25 per person for the right to vote in the election. Unfortunately, Jill E. Smere doesn't have $25. She wants to vote anyway. Refer to page 36, and to the 24th amendment on page 43. Does your current constitution deal with the issue of poll taxes? If so, how? If not, you will need to amend your constitution: _____
_____
_____

3. After 30 years of serving in office, President Drake U. Law has been diagnosed with a treatable form of cancer. He will need surgery and treatment, and will be in the hospital for several weeks. In the meantime he is very weak and is confined to his bed. He is in so much pain that he requires strong medication. Doctors feel confident that he will recover, but for the next few months, he will be laid up. Refer to page 36, and to the 25th amendment on page 43. Does your current constitution deal with issues of presidential disability? If so, how? If not, you will need to amend your constitution: _____
_____
_____

4. The Sophomore class from Punkville High has been studying the constitution in class. They decide to head for the election polls to demand the right to vote. Refer to the 26th amendment on page 43. Does your current constitution deal with issues of voting age? If so, how? If not, you will need to amend your constitution: _____
_____

5. Twelve senators decide they want a raise. They decide to give themselves a hefty raise of $150,000 a year. Refer to page 36, and to the 27th amendment. Does your current constitution deal with issues of pay raises for congressmen? If so, how? If not, you will need to amend your constitution: _____
_____
_____
_____

Amendments to the Constitution

Amendments, continued

Amendments, continued

Appendix

Notes on page 4 – Many organizations use acronyms as their names. An acronym is a word in which each letter stands for a word. One student taking this course called his organization "SAM's Club," which stood for "Sons of AMerica Club." Or, you might simply want to come up with a catchy name, such as this name coined by another student: "Justice R Us."

Notes on page 6 – You may make up an "ideal" person, or you may choose a person you know (such as your pastor or your dad). You may want to consider people in the news (such as President Bush) or people in history. One student chose Elvis! Why? He said Elvis could get people excited and enthusiastic! What do you think?

Notes on page 9 and 12 – Choose an organization that is known for fighting for "freedom" such as the ACLU (American Civil Liberties Union). Or, make up a name for their organization. Use the following points to help present *their* case (the points correspond to the questions on your sheet):
- Their interpretation of the law would explain what they have against you, and why you are in court.
- They want to protect their own freedoms. What freedoms of theirs have you and your organization violated?
- Any case must have evidence. What do they have on you? Pictures? Finger prints? Store receipts? Eye witnesses?
- Since they are trying to strengthen their organization, are there new "freedoms" they want?
- If they win, they'll want to restrict you from interfering further. What law would they like to pass to do this?

Notes on pages 10 and 13 – Now for your side. Use the following points to help you present *your* case (the points correspond with the questions on your worksheet):
- How do you interpret the law that made you confident that your organization's methods were permissible?
- Since they are trying to restrict you, what freedoms are they attacking that you would like to keep intact?
- They have presented evidence against you. How do you explain the evidence?
- Since the law is currently on their side, what freedoms are you hoping to establish or strengthen if you win?
- If you win, how will you keep them from suing you again? What restrictions would you like to impose on them?

Notes on pages 15 and 17 – When choosing a picture of your candidate, look for someone who looks "gubernatorial." You may pick a picture of someone you know (grandpa, brother) or a famous person (Abe Lincoln), or just pick a photo of a stranger from a magazine who looks the part.

Notes on pages 18 and 23 – This lesson is tricky. It is not the purpose of this project to stir up rebellion against your country in your heart. However, you should understand (think creatively!) what our Founding Fathers sacrificed for our sakes. Remind yourself of Romans 13:1 and 1 Timothy 2:1-2. For this reason, you may want to use and imaginary country for your "mother country." The exercise on page 22 involves mapping out your new country, and it includes a map of the United States. Why don't you take this opportunity to pray for our country and its leaders, and offer thanksgiving to God for all the ways He has blessed you as a citizen of this country. Please keep in mind that the objective of these exercises is as follows:
- To become familiar with the people and events surrounding the birth of this nation,
- To appreciate the great documents that guarantee our freedom,
- To be thankful for the sacrifices our Founding Fathers made in our behalf,
- To give glory to God for the amazing things He has done in the formation of this country,
- To learn to pray seriously for our country and its leaders.

Notes on page 22 – This exercise may be easier if you refer to physical, political, and population maps of the United States.

Notes on page 26 – Students seem to find this exercise difficult. Try to keep the bigger picture in mind while you are working. Remember, you are trying to win both support *and* freedom. The organizations listed are assets you can use to achieve this goal. As an example, if you lower tolls on your turnpikes, you might gain support. However, if you eliminate tolls altogether, you might gain the support of the people, but you won't have the finances necessary to repair your roads. Another example would be to ease up on pollution controls (such as emissions, aerosol sprays, dumping, etc.). You need to decide whether easing up on regulations would benefit or harm you. Memorializing fallen heroes may gain the good will of the people, but where will the money come from to build it? How can use the internet, postal systems, and education systems to promote freedom and gain support and unity? Think through this list of assets carefully, and utilize each to its fullest potential for God's glory and for your people.

Notes on page 28 – Why are alliances formed? During the Persian Gulf War, by allying with Kuwait, the US gained economically (oil) and politically (friendship with an Islamic nation). Kuwait gained political freedom. Israel and Kuwait both benefited technologically (military defense). In the Afghanistan conflict, the US gains in the area of "domestic tranquility" (decrease of terrorism) while Afghanistan gains religiously and politically as the Taliban is overthrown.

Notes on page 36 – You have essentially already written your constitution, but the pieces of it are spread over 2 pages. You must now piece it together. First, you'll want to copy your preamble (question 1, page 34). Next, you will write out your first article. The information you need for **Article 1** was introduced in question 3, page 34, and refined in question 1, page 35. Reword this information (if necessary), and recopy the information to create the first article of your constitution. Continue to go back and forth between pages 34 and 35 to create the rest of your constitution. You may need to reword your responses on page 34 to form complete sentences for your constitution. As an example, the question is asked, "If you have a legislative branch, how many houses will it have?" Suppose you answered: 2 . "What are the names of your houses?" Suppose you answered: senate, house of representatives. Now you will need to reword the information for the final draft of your constitution. Here is an example: "The legislative branch of government shall be made up of two houses, the Senate, and the House of Representatives."

Notes on page 37 – Yes, you have to create another candidate. Your first candidate was to be elected under the old system in order to bring about change. *This* candidate will be the first leader of your new nation.

Notes for lesson 14 – Each day for the next 6 days, you will be amending your constitution. The process is simple. You will read a description of a situation that has arisen in your country. You will check the constitution you wrote on page 36 to see if it deals with that particular situation. If it doesn't, you will need to amend your constitution. You can get ideas by looking at the paraphrased amendments of the United States Constitution (pages 42-43). By the end of the 6th day, you will have worked "the kinks" out of your constitution. You will compile your notes into a single document of constitutional amendments on the 7th day.

Day 1 (page 44) – All the changes you make in your constitution today will go into forming your first amendment. What are the dangers, if any, of restricting freedom. For example, if you want to mandate "Christianity" as the national religion, how will you define "Christianity"? Remember, Baptists, Amish, Charismatics, Lutherans, Jehovah Witnesses, Mormons, Catholics, and Mennonites all claim the title of "Christian". You will need to think through issues of free speech. Though most people agree that obscene language is wrong, what about speaking about "the gift of tongues" or "dating" instead of "courtship"? What about disrespectful language or talking about "Santa"? If you decide to draw a line regarding free speech, where will you draw it? This same thought process must be applied to issues of the press and assembly.

Day 2 (page 45) – We again have to decide whether or not to restrict or guarantee a freedom – the right to keep and bear arms (Q#1). Will you draw that line? If you do restrict that right, where will you draw the line? What will be the result if you do or don't restrict the right? What about issues of search and seizure (Q#3)? Is it ever okay? If so, how will you define it? How can the government abuse restriction? Think it through. What about private property (Q#4)? Will your government ever, under any circumstance, be able to take or purchase a person's property against his will? If so, what are the guidelines? Lastly, what about vigilante groups (Q#5)? Do your citizens have the right to take matters into their own hands? If so, under what circumstances?

Day 3 (page 46) – Today you will switch gears a little to think about some different issues. Litigation (suing) has gotten out of control in the country (Q#1). How will your constitution deal with this issue: allow or restrict? What will be the result? Next, you'll need to think about criminal punishment – what will you allow? Is prison effective? What about whipping? Public humiliation? What does the Bible say? What works in other countries? Has the prison system worked in our country? Think it through. In the third question, you'll need to address the possibility that your constitution hasn't addressed *all* the rights of your citizens. Think of the current "rights" being pushed in this country (some *are* valid): the right to life, the right to choose, equal rights for women, and gay rights. If your constitution missed a "right," does that mean that the right is invalid?

Next, you will deal with states' rights. Does your nation have states? Check what you wrote in article 4 of your constitution worksheet on page 34. If you do have states, how much power do they have? If you don't have states, then you won't need to amend your constitution on this point. The final situation also deals with states' rights.

Day 4 (Day 47) – Today brings up an interesting issue. Will slavery of any kind be permitted in your new nation (Q#2)? What about prisoners being assigned to hard labor? In the Bible, a destitute person can sell himself into slavery. In colonial days, children could be bound as apprentices, laboring in exchange for an education.

The final situation (Q#5) deals with the tax system. You already addressed this on page 39. Use the information you wrote there to create your amendment.

Day 5 (Day 48) – Prohibition (Q#2) is the next topic. The US tried to prohibit alcohol, but matters got worse. So, they granted the right to buy and drink alcohol to the people again. Will you try to restrict alcohol? If so, to what extent? What about smoking and drugs?

The final situation on Day 5 deals with term limits. The US limited presidential terms so that no one could ever become too powerful over a long period of time. Many people believe that these term limits should be eliminated so that a good president can keep being re-elected. What do you think?

Day 6 (Day 49) – The first situation on this page deals with the people who live in your nation's capital. Washington DC doesn't "belong" to any state, as it was thought that the state "owning" the capital might have more power than other states. The problem was that the capital's citizens couldn't vote, nor were they represented. What about your capital?

The second situation deals with poll tax. Can officials charge people for the right to vote? The final question deals with pay raises. Congressmen should be eligible for occasional pay raises, but who sets the raise? What are the guidelines?

Day 7 (Day 50-52) – You will need to compile all your amendments into a single document. You will also want to consider other amendments (women's rights, the right to life, gay rights, educational choice, etc.), and whether you want to grant, restrict, or deny the rights. Whereas the US Constitution currently has 27 amendments, your constitution may have more or less amendments.